GLOBETROTTERS

AUSTRIA

Jane Hinchey

First Published 2021 by
Redback Publishing
PO Box 357 Frenchs Forest NSW 2086
Australia

www.redbackpublishing.com
orders@redbackpublishing.com

ISBN 978-1-922322-27-2

Author: Jane Hinchey
Editor: Marlene Vaughan
Design: Redback Publishing

Original illustrations © Redback Publishing 2021
Originated by Redback Publishing

Printed and bound in China

Acknowledgements
Abbreviations: l—left, r—right, b—bottom, t—top, c—centre, m—middle
We would like to thank the following for permission to reproduce
photographs: (Images © shutterstock, wikimediacommons) p4br Karl Allen Lugmayer,

p5ml Fabio Lotti, p9ml Giannis Papanikos, p9tr Minoli, p10tr annie_zhak, p10bl aijaphoto, p12tl
BAHDANOVICH ALENA, p12br Sodel Vladyslav, p13br Jack Krier, p14bl photo-oxser, p15mr Timelynx,
p17tl neftali, p17tc Resul Muslu, p17br Li Sun, p18br Evannovostro, p20cm Renata Sedmakova, p21ml
photo.ua, p21mr Mitzo, p22bl Dave Z, p23tr Olga Popova, p23bl Everett Collection, p23br Everett
Collection, p24br Anibal Trejo, p27ml karamysh, p27br Giannis Papanikos

Every effort has been made to contact copyright holders of any material reproduced in this
book. Any omissions will be rectified in subsequent printings if notice is given to the publisher.

Disclaimer
All the internet addresses (URLs) given in this book were valid at the time of going to press.
However, due to the dynamic nature of the internet, some addresses may have changed, or
sites may have changed or ceased to exist since publication. While the author and publisher
regret any inconvenience this may cause readers, no responsibility for any such changes can
be accepted by either the author or the publisher.

A catalogue record for this
book is available from the
National Library of Australia

MIX
Paper from
responsible sources
FSC® C020056

CONTENTS

MAP OF AUSTRIA

Hallstatt
UPPER AUSTRIA

Schonbrunn Palace
VIENNA

CZECH REPUBLIC

● Linz

Vienna ●

● Salzburg

GERMANY

● Innsbruck

Graz ●

SLOVAKIA

LIECHTENSTEIN

SWITZERLAND

ITALY

HUNGARY

SLOVENIA

Melk Abbey
MELK

Hochosterwitz Castle
CARINTHIA

Eisriesenwelt
WERFERN

Vienna city
VIENNA

Krems
WACHAU

SNAPSHOT

COUNTRY

Republik Österreich
(Republic of Austria)

CAPITAL

Vienna

OFFICIAL LANGUAGE

German

AREA

83,879
square kilometres

POPULATION

9,000,000
(2020)

RELIGIONS Roman Catholic, Protestant, Muslim, Jewish, Christian Orthodox

CURRENCY Euro

Find them on a map!

AUSTRIA SHARES LAND BORDERS WITH EIGHT OTHER COUNTRIES. THEY ARE:

- Czech Republic • Slovakia • Slovenia
- Hungary • Switzerland
- Liechtenstein • Germany
- Italy

WELCOME TO AUSTRIA

Krimml waterfalls
AUSTRIAN ALPS

Officially known as the Republic of Austria, Österreich is a small, landlocked country located in Central Europe. It is a mountainous country, with the Alps dominating the landscape and the mighty Danube River snaking its way right through. Forests cover more than 46 per cent of the country's total area.

The region has been inhabited for tens of thousands of years. Austria is a stable country politically, with a rich and vibrant cultural life and high standard of living.

Austria's Nine states

1. Burgenlandt
2. Carinthia
3. Lower Austria
4. Upper Austria
5. Salzburg
6. Styria
7. Tyrol
8. Vorarlberg
9. Vienna

Government

Austria is a federal parliamentary democratic republic, meaning its citizens elect a party and President, who then decides who will be the next Chancellor. The Chancellor is the head of government but has no real political power.

Austria's nine independent federal regions have their own provincial governments.

The Austrian Parliament Building
VIENNA

The President lives and works at Hofburg Imperial Palace

Did You Know?

In 1955, Austria passed the Declaration of Neutrality, declaring the country permanently neutral, meaning they don't take sides in conflicts or form military alliances.

7

Natural Resources:

Austria's resources include magnesite, tungsten, timber, arable land, lignite, iron ore, copper, nickel, salt and hydropower.

Agriculture:

Austria produces crops such as grain, wheat, barley, oats, rye, corn (maize), potatoes, beets, grapes and other fruit, wine, as well as cattle, pigs and poultry.

Main Industries:

Austria's most important industry is tourism. Other industries include making machinery, metallurgical products and textiles.

Hallstatt is a famous tourist town

The predominant ethnic group in Austria, ethnic-Austrians, descends from the Germanic people of Northern Europe, and were identified by the Romans as speakers of German languages. But don't confuse Austrians with Germans, despite their shared history. Modern Austrians date back to Hapsburg rule in the 16th century.

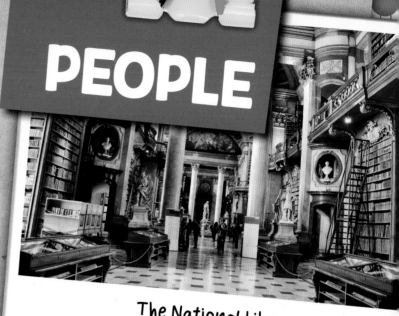

The National Library
HOFBURG PALACE

Cafe Central
VIENNA

Austria has nine regional provinces, each with its own distinct character and traits. Austrians from Tyrol or Burgenland are very different to the Viennese. Some regions have close links to the country they border. Depending on the region, there will be old customs and traditions that are still practised today. Traditional dress exists in some areas, although it is largely reserved for official ceremonies and festivals.

Around 20 per cent of the country's population lives in the capital, Vienna. The Viennese are considered to be sophisticated and cultured.

The majority of the population is ethnic Austrian and speaks German. Other languages spoken include Croatian, Hungarian and Slovene.

There are six other ethnic groups officially recognised in Austria:

- Burgenlandic Croatians
- Roma
- Slovaks
- Slovenians
- Czechs
- Hungarians

Czech boys and girls dance in traditional dress at a folklore festival

Austria is also home to many immigrant groups.

Traditional Dress

Traditional dress is called 'tracht' and varies in some regions, but the most well known is the 'dirndl' for women and the 'lederhosen' for men. The dirndl consists of a pinafore dress, with a blouse and apron. The lederhosen are leather trousers, worn with a shirt.

DAILY LIFE

In Austria, family is very important. Most households consist of just one family, but it is common for extended family to come together to share special occasions.

Going skiing is a popular way to spend a vacation

Austrians savour their leisure time and cultural pursuits. All over the country, people belong to cultural and sports clubs. They are entitled to 25 days vacation, making Austria one of the best countries in the world for paid leave. Many people take their leave over the summer.

Good Manners!

Etiquette is highly regarded. In Austria, it's polite to always be punctual.

Two thirds of Austria's population live in cities or towns. The most heavily populated city is Vienna.

WHERE AUSTRIANS LIVE

Albertina Museum
VIENNA

Cities and Towns

Austrians who live in cities or urban areas enjoy a high quality of life. Residents have access to excellent infrastructure, shopping, markets and restaurants. People play sport, visit galleries and museums and attend events. Families can choose from good school and medical facilities, and children have quite a lot of freedom and independence from a young age.

The Capital – Vienna

Vienna is home to over 20 per cent of Austria's population, and is consistently voted one of the world's most liveable cities. The standard of living is high for most Viennese. Public transport is excellent, as is education and healthcare. It is a city of the arts, with great music events and festivals, and world class museums and galleries. It has an unsurpassed 'coffee house' culture and restaurant scene, abundant parks and paths along the Danube, and in summer locals embrace the outdoors. Vienna is beautiful, with a glorious history of which the locals are proud.

Locals enjoying summer
DANUBE RIVER

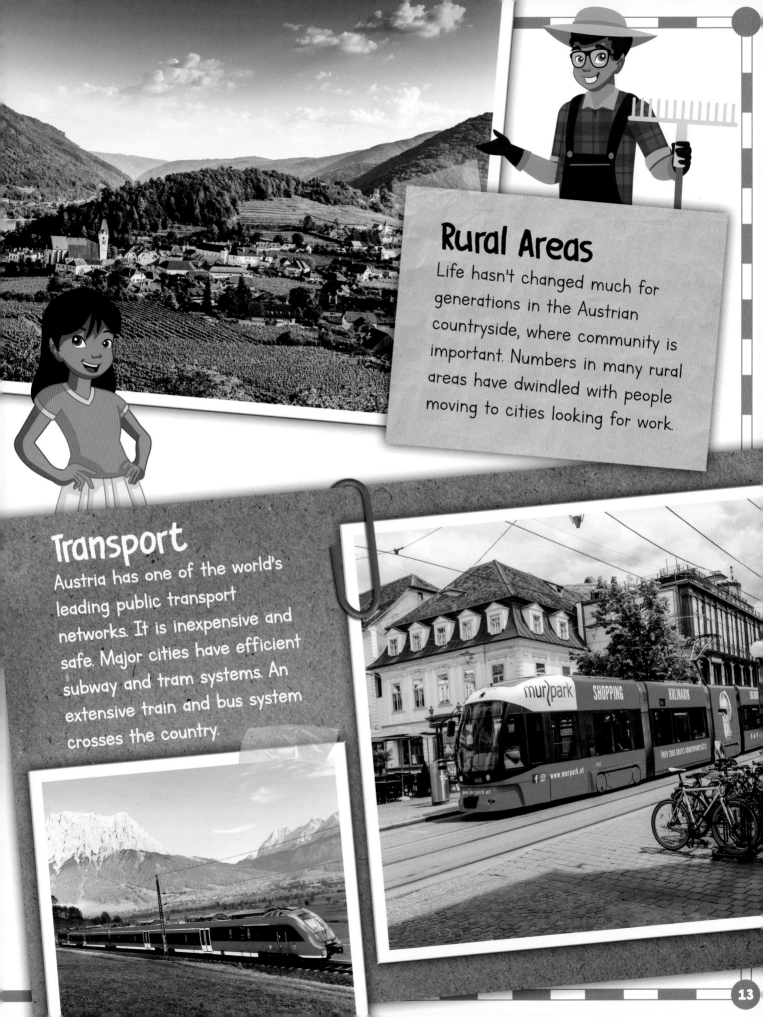

Rural Areas

Life hasn't changed much for generations in the Austrian countryside, where community is important. Numbers in many rural areas have dwindled with people moving to cities looking for work.

Transport

Austria has one of the world's leading public transport networks. It is inexpensive and safe. Major cities have efficient subway and tram systems. An extensive train and bus system crosses the country.

A LOVE OF WINTER SPORTS

Austrians love sport. Due to the alpine terrain, snow sports are extremely popular. Skiing, snowboarding and other winter sports are not only popular with locals, but account for a major share of tourism, with visitors coming from all over the world to ski.

Other popular sports are ice-hockey, motor sports, tennis and football.

LINZ
VIENNA
SALZBURG
INNSBRUCK
GRAZ

Austria vs Hungary ice hockey game

EDUCATION

Austria's education system is one of the best in Europe, and school is mandatory and free. Children attend school from age six to sixteen. While the government oversees some aspects of education, schools and the curriculum are mostly state run. There are different stages, from elementary to secondary school, and also tertiary opportunities.

The school day begins early, often around 7.30 am, but finishes early afternoon. Children attend various extracurricular activities in the afternoon. The school year starts in August each year, after the six week summer break.

The Federal Ministry of Education is responsible for funding and supervising schools, while education is administered by the respective states.

A class of Viennese students go on a field trip

THE ARTS

Austria has produced many of the world's great artists, writers and musicians.

The Secession Building
VIENNA

Art Scene

The Vienna Secession movement was a group of artists who rejected the academic art style of the late 19th century. The founding member of the movement was Gustav Klimt, one of the most influential figures in art of that time. His style is distinctive due to his use of mosaic and dazzling gold leaf. His painting, The Kiss, is a celebration of love, and is now one of the world's most famous and easily recognisable artworks.

Portrait of Adele Bloch-Bauer I

The Kiss

Statue of Mozart
BURGGARTEN, VIENNA

Music to My Ears!

Austria is the birthplace of some of the world's most famous musicians. Franz Joseph Haydn, Johann Strauss, and Franz Schubert were all Austrian.

One of the world's most famous composers was Wolfgang Amadeus Mozart, who was born in Salzburg. During his life he composed 50 symphonies, 22 operas and many other works. He died in poverty aged 35. It wasn't until after his death that his music won acclaim.

The Vienna Boys Choir

For nearly 500 years, every Sunday the Vienna Boys Choir has sung solemn mass in the Hofburg Chapel. Today, tourists can listen to them sing at the many performances they hold throughout the year.

HUNDERTWASSER HOUSE

The Hundertwasser House in Vienna is one of Austria's top tourist attractions and an architectural highlight. It is an apartment block containing apartments, offices, private terraces and communal terraces, which can only be viewed from the outside.

The Hundertwasser House is designed with uneven lines, uneven windows and a colourful, patchwork exterior. The designer, Friedensreich Hundertwasser, had also planned to have uneven floors, but for practical reasons this didn't happen.

Construction began on the public housing building in 1983. When it was completed in 1985, it received a great deal of criticism, but it quickly became a popular destination for locals and tourists alike. Now, with its trees and shrubs planted on balconies and the roof, it is a colourful, chaotic oasis of nature and art in the city.

Hundertwasser Village

Opposite the Hundertwasser House is the Hundertwasser Village, which is open to visitors. Hundertwasser created the village in a tyre workshop in 1990-1991. There are a number of stores, cafes and bars in the typical Hundertwasser style.

LANGUAGE

Learn the Lingo

German is a West Germanic language, along with English and Dutch. More than 120 million people in Austria, Germany, Switzerland, Luxembourg, Liechtenstein and in parts of Belgium, Northern Italy and Eastern France speak German.

Danke
Thank you

Guten morgen
Good morning

Ja
Yes

Sprechen sie Englisch?
Do you speak English?

Nein
No

Bitte
Please

Entschuldigen sie
Excuse me

Guten abend
Good evening

Minority Languages
A number of minority languages are officially recognised in Austria.

- 2.4 per cent of Austrians speak Serbian.
- 2.3 per cent of the population speak Turkish.
- Hungarian is spoken in Burgenland.
- Burgenland Croatian is spoken in the Burgenland province.
- Slovene is an official language in Carinthia.

RELIGION

Approximately 64 per cent of Austrians are Roman Catholic, followed by around 5 per cent who are Protestant. There are smaller Muslim, Christian Orthodox, and Jewish communities. Around 12 per cent of Austrian people don't follow any religion.

Beautiful Churches

Austria has many beautiful churches and cathedrals. One of the most important is St Stephen's Cathedral in Vienna. First constructed in the 12th century, it is the most important Gothic church in the country and has the second biggest free-swinging bell in Europe.

The gothic interior of St Stephen's Cathedral

St Stephen's Cathedral
VIENNA

The Venus of Willendorf

In 1908, in the village of Willendorf, archaeologist Josef Szombathy discovered a small statue that dates to between 24,000 - 22,000 BC, making it one of the oldest and most famous surviving works of art.

The area that is today Austria has a long, rich history. From around 400 BC it was occupied by Celtic tribes who built a village where Vienna is today. Around 30 BC, the Celts were conquered by Roman invaders.

Hapsburg Rule

In 1276, Rudolf I was the first Hapsburg to rule. He was from one of Europe's most powerful imperial families. The Hapsburgs were very important in European history, ruling Austria and later Austria-Hungary for more than 700 years. During this time, Austria was one of the most important centres of power in Europe.

Statue of Emperor Charles VI
AUSTRIAN NATIONAL LIBRARY

Empress Maria Theresa

One of the great Hapsburg monarchs was Empress Maria Theresa who ruled from 1740 to 1780, successfully fighting off many attempts to overthrow her during this time. She is recognised as a great ruler who promoted education and reformed the legal system. She was the only female head of the Hapsburgs, and mother to 16 children. One of her daughters was Marie Antionette, who married Louis XVI of France in 1770 and who was executed by guillotine during the French revolution.

First World War

Archduke Franz Ferdinand was heir to the Austro-Hungarian throne. On June 28, 1914 he was assassinated in Sarajevo. In response, Austria-Hungary declared war on Serbia. By August 5, Europe was at war, as Great Britain, Russia and France formed an alliance, known as the 'Triple Entente', against Germany and Austria-Hungary.

Hitler and the Holocaust

Adolf Hitler was born in Austria and became the leader of Nazi Germany. He was responsible for the Holocaust and instrumental in starting the Second World War when he ordered the invasion of Poland. Hitler believed in a pure Germanic race of people, so minority races were persecuted, particularly the Jews.

The Nazis deported thousands of Jews from Austria. Many were sent to concentration camps. By 1942, only around 7,000 Jews remained in Austria.

Austrians celebrate many important days, festivals and events throughout the year.

Christmas

Christmas is an important religious celebration in Austria. The festive season begins with the Advent celebrations on the fourth Sunday before Christmas Day. Families decorate an Advent wreath with four red candles. December 6 is St Nicholas Day, when children get gifts or sweets in their shoes. In some regions, a horned monster called 'Knecht Ruprecht'

or 'Krampus' accompanies 'Nikolaus' to punish children who have been naughty.

Families gather together on Christmas Eve when the Christmas tree is lit. During the festive season, cities and towns are draped in decorations and lights and many hold annual Christmas markets. The markets are filled with stalls that sell artisan goods and foods such as sugar cookies, roasted chestnuts and hot, mulled wine.

Ball Season

The Viennese invented the waltz. Every winter, over 400 balls are held in Vienna, with the most famous being the Vienna Opera Ball, held at the beautiful State Opera House.

FOOD

Austrian food incorporates influences from nearby neighbours including Germany and Hungary. The cuisine also varies from region to region.

Rich soil provides abundant grains, fruits and vegetables. Meat such as pork, beef, poultry, venison and rabbit is a staple, as well as freshwater fish.

In Austria, cheeses and bread are often eaten at breakfast. Salad accompanies most meals.

Apple strudel is a popular dessert made all around the country

Mealtimes are important and seen as a time to relax, savour food and enjoy the company of others.

ON THE MENU

Wiener Schnitzel: considered to be Austria's national dish, this crumbed veal cutlet is now popular all over the world.

Wiener Würstel: Austrians love their sausages. Types of sausage may vary from region to region, but are commonly eaten with potato salad and radishes. They are a popular meal from street vendors.

Kartoffelpuffer: a fried potato pancake often served with eggs for breakfast.

Sachertorte: one of the most famous chocolate cakes in the world, made with dense sponge cake and thin layers of apricot jam that's topped with a semi-firm chocolate icing.

Brezel: large dough pretzels sold everywhere in Austria.

Have you eaten any of these Austrian foods?

CAFÉ CULTURE

The Viennese take their cafes so seriously that 'Viennese Coffee House Culture' is listed as 'Intangible Cultural Heritage' in the National Agency for the Intangible Cultural Heritage (a part of UNESCO). The Viennese coffee house is described as a place, 'where time and space are consumed, but only the coffee is found on the bill.'

There are many famous cafes in Vienna. Their customers include royalty, musicians, composers and artists. Freud and Jung often sat in cafes with other intellectuals of their time. But the most legendary cafe for writers, philosophers and poets has always been Café Central. Today it remains a popular Viennese cafe and tourist destination.

Inside the famous cafe central
VIENNA

GEOGRAPHY AND CLIMATE

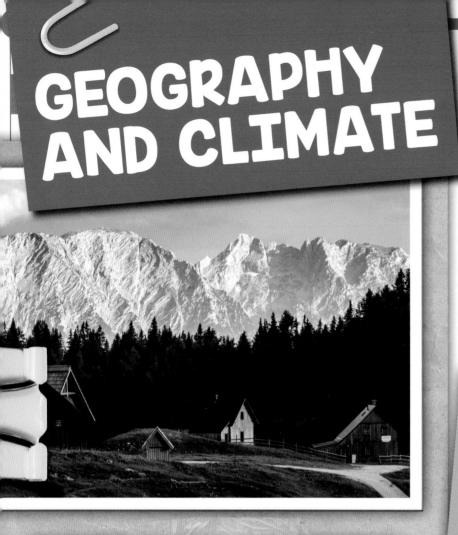

Austria is a landlocked country covering 83,879 square kilometres. It is bordered by the Czech Republic, Slovakia, Slovenia, Hungary, Switzerland, Liechtenstein and Germany. It has diverse geography, including soaring mountains, vast forests and a flat plateau in the north. Ten per cent of the country is alpine terrain, making it unsuitable for agriculture.

Climate

Climate varies depending on the region, but is generally temperate. The warmest temperatures are during July and August, although it can still be mild. Winters can be cold and cloudy.

The Austrian Alps

Dramatic and beautiful, Austria's main geographical feature, the Alps, cross the country from east to west. Formed more than 30 million years ago, the Austrian Alps are divided into three mountain ranges. The highest peak is the Grossglockner.

Austria is famous for its valleys, forests, and more than 300 sparkling lakes. It has some of the most beautiful summer hiking trails in Europe. In winter, visitors flock to ski resorts.

The Danube

The Danube River enters Austria from Germany and stretches 349 kilometres through the country, with 96 per cent of Austria drained by the river and its tributaries.

Wildflowers
MOUNT GROSSGLOCKNER

Forests and Flora

Austria is one of Europe's most heavily wooded countries, with an abundance of trees such as larch, oak, beech, fir and pine. Wildflower species bloom from late June through early August in the alpine meadows. Flowers include gentian, alpine carnation, arnica, alpine rose, heather and the protected edelweiss.

Environmental Protection

The environment has always been important to Austrians, and their country is one of the world leaders in sustainability. Around 20 per cent of all farming is organic, and small-scale farms are thriving. Almost half of Austria's federal territory is covered by forests. Cities have sustainable development programs, and Austrians are well ahead of the world in being responsible for their own carbon footprint.

WILDLIFE

Austria has a diverse array of wildlife. Deer, fox, hare, badger, beaver, wading birds and wild boar are common. Lynx, chamoix, the ibex and the golden eagle live in the Alps.

The Eurasian lynx

A European badger swimming

In the alpine region, conservationists have been working on the return of large carnivores, such as the wolf, bear and lynx, which all disappeared from Austria, as well as on the protection of the last pristine natural and wild areas of the Alps. After they were poached to extinction in the region, Austria is now home again to a small bear population.

The golden eagle

FLAG AND SYMBOLS

National Anthem

The national anthem of Austria is named 'Land der Berge, Land am Strome', which means, 'Land of mountains, land by the river'.

Flag

Austria's national flag consists of three equal horizontal bands in red, white and red. The two red stripes denote strength and bravery, while white symbolises truth and honesty.

Coat of Arms

Austria's Coat of Arms is a black eagle with a yellow beak, crown, and claws. The eagle holds a sickle and a hammer in its talons with a broken handcuff chain.

National Flower

Austria's national flower is the edelweiss.

National Animal

Austria's national animal is the black eagle.

GLOSSARY

culture practices, beliefs and customs of a society or people

dialect variation of a language unique to a region

ethnic group people who share a common culture, language and heritage

Holocaust from the Greek word 'holokauston', meaning 'sacrifice by fire'. It refers to the Nazi persecution and slaughter of the Jewish people and others

immigrant person who settles in another country

Nazi German acronym standing for 'Nationalsozialistishe Deutsche Arbeiterpartei' ('National Socialist German Workers' Party')

walz three-step dance with formal steps and twirling

INDEX

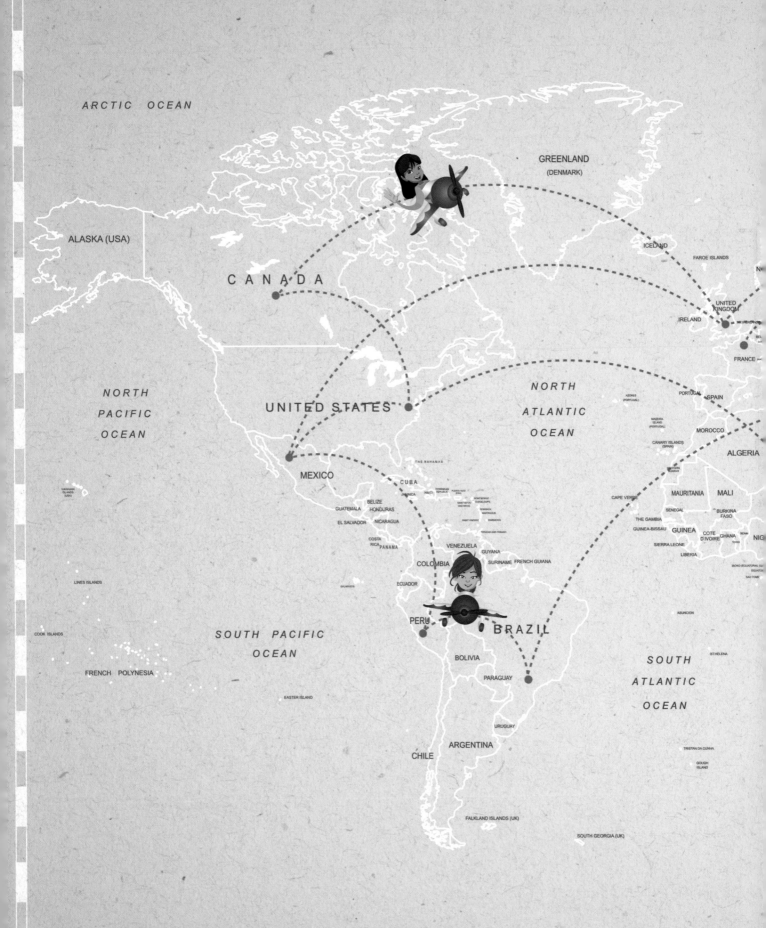